THE BREAKER
ANOINTING

GOD'S POWER TO
PRESS THROUGH

THE BREAKER
ANOINTING

GOD'S POWER TO
PRESS THROUGH

BARBARA J. YODER

WAGNER
PUBLICATIONS

The Breaker Anointing
Copyright © 2001 by Barbara J. Yoder
ISBN 1-58502-017-6

Published by
Wagner Publications
11005 N. Highway 83, Colorado Springs, Colorado 80921
www.wagnerpublications.org

Edit and interior design by Rebecca Sytsema

Rights for publishing this book in other languages are contracted by Gospel Literature International (GLINT). GLINT also provides technical help for the adaptation, translation, and publishing of Bible study resources and books in scores of languages worldwide. For further information, contact GLINT, P.O. Box 4060, Ontario, CA 91761-1003, USA. You may also send e-mail to glintint@aol.com, or visit their web site at www.glint.org.

1 2 3 4 5 6 7 8 9   07 06 05 04 03 02 01

CONTENTS

Foreword

by Chuck D. Pierce

The book you now hold in your hands contains essential lessons that are important for any Christian! Why? Because it is the anointing that breaks the yoke of what is holding us back from entering all that God has for us.

Why, for example, do we get so far in our prayer life and never see a manifestation of God's promise? How can we understand the anointing that breaks us into a fulfillment of God's purposes for our lives? Barbara Yoder does an excellent job of explaining how the glory of God breaks through into our lives and cities to bring change. Her premise comes from Micah 2:13 which says, "The one who breaks open will come up before them; they will break out, pass through the gate, and go out by it ..."

There is a tremendous warfare that is going on at the gates of our cities. Only the breaker anointing can cause us to break through the demonic forces that control the entry way of God's presence and bring true change into our lives, our cities, and

our regions.   As you read this book, you can expect that there
will be a "lifting of your head"; for as you come to understand the breaker anointing and the manifestation of God as
the Breaker, God will begin to pass before you and break
open a new way.   Get ready to have a marked increase in both
your understanding and your faith in God's ability to break
through any gate that is standing in your way!

Chuck D. Pierce
President, Glory of Zion International Ministries, Inc.
Denton, Texas

Vice President, Global Harvest Ministries
Colorado Springs, Colorado

CHAPTER ONE:

MY INTRODUCTION TO THE BREAKER

In 1970 I moved from Wisconsin to Detroit, Michigan to do graduate work at Wayne State University. When I got there a friend of mine invited me to go with her to her church, Bethesda Missionary Temple. I ended up in what was, for me, a very unusual church service. It was not like anything I had ever experienced in my days of growing up in traditional, evangelical churches.

Several things about this service amazed me, capturing my complete, though skeptical, attention. People sang intensely in a way I knew they were totally engaged. When they clapped their hands, it seemed too much to me. I felt they trivialized the awesomeness of God. If that wasn't enough, they then raised their hands! I was just about ready to get out of there when something happened.

People began to spontaneously sing praises to the Lord individually and independent of each other or any corporately led song. I had never heard anything like that. It was as if angels were present in that place and singing with them. Suddenly the same presence of the Lord returned to me that I experienced the night of my conversion experience. Because of that "happening," I found myself going back to the church weekly even though I did not understand what was happening. Something had "broken through" the hardness of my intellectual shell.

Rev. Myrtle D. Beall founded and pastored that church of 3,500 people. She was an amazing woman that was around 80 years of age. Every Sunday morning, someone rolled her wheelchair up to the podium and she spoke to the congregation. Many things were imparted into my spirit, which I did not fully understand with my mind.

Unable to Break Through

One notable infrequent, unpredictable, and recurring event took place on some Sundays. The service would begin and we could feel something was not right. There was a tangible tightness, lid, heaviness, or oppression in the service. Though I was unable to explain it in words, I just knew that it seemed we could not get anywhere in the service. We were stuck.

I'll never forget the first time I experienced one of those Sundays. Suddenly someone rolled Pastor Beall's wheelchair to the podium. I wondered what was going on since it was not time for her to preach. There seemed to be an unusual fire and determination in her eyes and body posture. All of a sudden she stretched out her right arm toward the congregation and let out this loud, authoritative declaration, which went something like this, "HAAR—ROOSH!" I about jumped out of the seat. A hush settled over the congregation. Suddenly that sense of heaviness or lid was completely gone. People began to sing or break out in some way spontaneously.

Opening Up
the Spiritual Atmosphere

Little did I know that I had just experienced the "breaker anointing." Whatever it was, it opened up the spiritual atmosphere and a tangible release occurred. Every time the heaviness returned, Pastor Beall would release one of those powerful "HAAR—ROOSH" declarations and the atmosphere instantly changed.

Back in the '70s, we did not know about the breaker anointing. We just knew and believed that the anointing broke every yoke, as we learned in Isaiah 10:27. We therefore figured that these declarations were "the anointing" because they broke that which had bridled us.

The Breaker

We now know that it is the anointing, but it is more than that. Micah 2:13 says, "The breaker goes up before them; they break out, pass through the gate, and go out by it. So their king goes on before them, and the LORD at their head." (NAS) It is the "breaker anointing" coming into our midst. It is God manifesting Himself as the Breaker. One of His names then is, God the Breaker.

Under the tutelage of Pastor Myrtle D. Beall, I grew up spiritually in an environment where the manifestation of God as the Breaker was frequent. Approximately 450 to 500 alcoholics were set free under her ministry. People who wanted to change experienced the power of God to break them out of old habit patterns and bondages into freedom. Those were awesome days. We went from freedom to greater freedom both individually and corporately.

There at Bethesda, the love of God was demonstrated in power through Jesus Christ when He set captives free. Those who were captivated and broken down by devastating life experiences were changed and released from prisons of fear (see Luke 4:18-19). This is a type of breaker anointing.

In Detroit, through Pastor Myrtle D. Beall, I was introduced to the power of the Breaker coming into the midst of the church both individually and corporately. However, the breaker anointing is not only for individuals; it is also corporate and territorial.

The Breaker Affects Corporate Structures of Churches and Cities

There is a territorial aspect to the breaker anointing. In his book *Informed Intercession*, George Otis, Jr. speaks about the territorial aspect of the breaker anointing. He calls it breakthrough and identifies it as the second phase of revival. First a beachhead is established, and then breakthrough occurs. Breakthrough is identified by the fact that a powerful, ruling evil presence over a territory has been broken. These breakthroughs remove hindrances to people perceiving the gospel and result in conversion. No longer do churches remain small and without influence. When the power is broken through in a territory, people start streaming into churches throughout the region. The churches begin to experience influence and respect in their territory.[1]

This book is about the Breaker and the breaker anointing. It is an anointing that affects individuals, churches, and cities.

When the breaker anointing comes into an area it results in changes not only in individuals but also in churches, the socio-political structure, and belief systems of the city. What started out in my life as a seemingly isolated and localized spiritual phenomenon has become a spiritual dynamic that should be usual and expected in the apostolic church. For individuals, churches, and cities to change, the breaker anointing must be an integral part of that transformation. The Breaker must come if we are to see widespread change in each of these areas.

Notes

[1] George Otis. Jr., *Informed Intercession*, (Ventura, CA: Renew Books, 1999), pp. 59, 66-69.

CHAPTER TWO:

RESTORATION OF
THE APOSTOLIC CHURCH

These are awesome days in which God is restoring the New Testament church written about in Acts, which is the apostolic church. Because this restoration is taking place within contemporary society, it differs culturally from the church in Acts. But it does not differ in the core of strength, power, wisdom, and motivating force, which for both is the empowerment by the Holy Spirit and our identity in Christ. This restoration will cause the church to arise and make great advancement in this hour. It is already happening in many countries around the world.

The Third Day Church

Many national and world leaders in Christendom are talking and writing about the restoration of the apostolic church. This restoration is transforming the face of the church from a passive, withdrawn entity into a bold, aggressive, and advancing spiritual force. Some refer to it as the Third Day Church. In his book *The Future War of the Church* (Renew Books), Chuck D. Pierce writes extensively about the Third Day Church. This reference is extracted from Hosea 6:1-2, which says, "Come, and let us return to the LORD; for He has torn, but He will heal us; he has stricken, but He will bind us up. After two days He will revive us; on the third day He will raise us up, that we may live in His sight."

In the second millennium, God was reviving us. He was bringing the church back to life. This was most obviously initiated when Martin Luther ignited the Protestant Reformation. That Reformation began to change the course of the church. Now we have entered the third millennium. Prophetically speaking, this third millennium is likened to the third day when Hosea said God would raise us up and we would live, not die. It is the Third Day Church which will restore apostolic authority and influence.

A prophetic picture of that raising up is expressed in Ezekiel 37 where Ezekiel began to prophesy to the valley of dead, dry and sun-bleached bones. Suddenly something miraculous began to happen. The bones began to create a noise as they came together and were re-formed into bodies. Then breath was breathed into them and they revived. When the life restoration process was completed, those restored people were transformed into a mighty army. They were not only revived but they arose to form a powerful corporate force. This is a also a picture of the Third Day Church. It is the army of God arising.

Today it is the church arising out of a culturally-entrenched and binding understanding of what it should be. That mindset has limited the ability of the church to affect society around it.

It seems that many are content just to restore people so that they have nice families and good children. The church has failed in the last generation to go on and radically affect society. In a sense, it has degenerated into a cultural mindset that has neutered the original mandate of the church. But now many are beginning to arise out of a place of death, awaken out of lethargy and sleepiness, and are consequently receiving true revelation over the core purpose of the church.

The church of Acts was a bold church led by apostles who partnered with prophets and teachers. It was not a passive church, which became so culturally entrapped and blinded that its ability to impact and transform society was hindered. We have sought to change society primarily through secondary change processes such as political means, rather than boldly declaring and establishing the gospel of Jesus Christ. We have tried to change society without first changing the soul of the church and the souls of men and women. However that has begun to change. We need both.

Restoration of the Apostolic Church and Mandate

God is restoring apostles, prophets, and teachers to their original destiny in the New Testament church. First Corinthians 12:28 speaks of the order of God in the church: "And God has appointed these in the church: first apostles, second prophets, third teachers, after that miracles, then gifts of healings, helps, administrations, varieties of tongues." When the church gets back in New Testament order, miracles, healing, and the rest of verse 28 will break out. When apostolic government is in order, miracles and healing occur. This is what is happening in many nations.

If we were to study the book of Acts to decipher the functions or mandate of apostles, we would see that apostles govern, exercise territorial authority (by breaking into new geographical territories that were previously unevangelized), reproduce or multiply themselves, build and establish the church, finish or complete what they have started, and send out believers to accomplish Kingdom purposes.

The original apostolic mandate was given in the Garden of Eden when God said to Adam and Eve in Genesis 1:28: "God blessed them, and God said to them, 'Be fruitful and multiply; fill the earth and subdue it; have dominion over the fish of the sea, over the birds of the air, and over every living thing that moves on the earth.'" God made the human race to be an apostolic people. The natural mindset of a Christian should be one that asks, "How can I bear fruit, multiply, fill the earth, subdue it for God, and exercise dominion over every living thing? In other words, how can I advance the kingdom of God?"

An Apostle Is "a Sent One"

The word for apostle in the Greek is *apostolos*, which means a delegate, specifically an ambassador of the gospel, commissioned by Christ with miraculous powers. Simply put, it is a "sent one" or one that is sent by God as differentiated from someone who decided on their own to go forth and accomplish something. The Greek verb *apostello* means to set apart, to send out on a mission.

Second Corinthians 12:12 speaks about the apostle and the power of God demonstrated through that office. One of the distinguishing marks of an apostle is miraculous power demonstrated through signs, wonders, and miracles. "Truly the signs of an apostle were accomplished among you with all perseverance, in signs and wonders and mighty deeds." Believers, though most are not apostles, are called to be an apostolic people. Given the Greek definition, an apostolic people are those who are called, set apart, and sent out by God to accomplish a specific mission with miraculous power. This statement can be taken apart and the elements determine the criteria for apostolic people: called by God, set apart, and sent out both by God and the governing authorities of the church, to accomplish a defined and specific mission or purpose. In accomplishing the goal, miraculous power will be demonstrated.

The Arising of a New Breed

The church in America, through a non-biblical paradigm, has evolved into a people who have been onlookers and bystanders. The professional clergy have been the ones responsible for seeing that the church advanced. However, with the change in paradigms through the restoration of the apostolic church, a new breed is arising.

This new breed believes the apostolic mandate and is arising with a seriousness about and faith in what the Word says about who they are. They have the heart of Jesus and are motivated by both the Great Commission and Luke 4:18-19. The Great Commission says, "Go therefore and make disciples of all the nations, baptizing them in the name of the Father and of the Son and of the Holy Spirit" (Matt. 28:19-20). The Bible further says, "And He said to them, 'Go into all the world and preach the gospel to every creature'" (Mark 16:15).

Luke 4:18-19 says, "The Spirit of the Lord is upon Me, because He has anointed Me to preach the gospel to the poor;

he has sent Me to heal the brokenhearted, to proclaim liberty to the captives and recovery of sight to the blind, to set at liberty those who are oppressed; To proclaim the acceptable year of the Lord."

This new breed of apostolic movers and shakers has a heart not just for individuals but also for cities and nations. They believe that God can change cities and nations just as He changes individuals. They are arising with faith, confidence, and bold courageous action.

The book of Acts makes it clear that the message of the apostolic church is the message of the Kingdom. Jesus talked about the level of intensity required to take the Kingdom. In Matthew 11:12, Jesus said, "from the days of John the Baptist until now the kingdom of heaven suffers violence, and the violent take it by force."

The Arising of Kingdom Movers and Shakers

What does that mean? Matthew 11:12 sounds like a group of angry people armed with guns and sophisticated weaponry. In *Strong's Greek and Hebrew Dictionary*, there are four related words for violence or violent which mean to force, to press, to crowd into, mighty, and energetic. *The Goodspeed Translation* says, "men have been taking the Kingdom of Heaven by storm." *Williams Translation* says "men are seizing it as a precious prize." Williams translated it this way: "these eager souls are storming it."

In other words, people who believe the gospel are taking seriously the apostolic mandate to press mightily and energetically into every area of society and the world, releasing the kingdom of heaven on earth. The kingdom of heaven will overtake and overthrow every other kingdom. There is a new breed arising through whom God will shake the earth. They will create a sound much like the one reflected in the title of a worship CD produced by Glory of Zion: "There's a Rumbling in the Heavens, There's a Rumbling in the Earth." Worship leader John Dickson and the worship team of Glory of Zion are one of the most prophetic teams in the nation, heralding on earth what is sounding forth in heaven.[1] It is the church giving birth to the new move that Dr. C. Peter Wagner refers to as The New Reformation.

A New Anointing Needed: The Breaker Anointing

To accomplish this mission, this breed of radical movers and shakers needs a new anointing. It is an anointing that will break through every obstacle and hindrance to the furtherance of the gospel and salvation of individuals and territories to the uttermost. God's intention is not a-little-dab-will-do-you type of breakthrough. It is a breakthrough that goes to the uttermost of who we are individually and corporately (see Heb. 7:25). It shakes everything loose that is holding back individuals as well as the church. It shakes the church out of the wilderness and into Canaan, the Promise, as we see in Psalm 29.

What is the anointing that is needed? It is the breaker anointing. The anointing essential to accomplishing the apostolic mandate is the breaker anointing. It is the hallmark anointing needed to reach the goal, to be an apostolic people boldly pressing forward and breaking through.

The breaker anointing is the anointing that breaks one through every *kairos* (opportune) challenge. Each season in

God that we enter has an opportune or *kairos* challenge. In
other words, God has something for us to break through which
will deliver us into the next season. Each season has a unique
challenge requiring a breakthrough in an area that has not been
broken through in past times. God wants to show up as the
Master of breakthroughs with the anointing to accomplish His
purposes for every new season in which He leads us.

Notes

[1] For information on obtaining a copy of the CD "There's a Rumbling in
the Heavens, There's a Rumbling in the Earth," contact Glory of Zion
Ministries toll-free at 1-888-965-1099 or send an e-mail to
GloryofZion22@aol.com.

CHAPTER THREE

GOD

THE BREAKER

We are moving out of an era of passive spectators filling churches led by pastors afraid to lead. We are leaving a time where the whole focus of the church has been individual or "me" focused. What is in this for me? How can I get help; how can I get blessed; how can I feel better; how can I, I, I, I, I . . .? There is a new church arising out of the heart of God that is led by apostles and prophets.

A Dilemma of Leaders

Pastors have often catered to the cries of people who are filled with fear and unbelief because of past wounds and hurts. In his book *The River Of Life*, Francis Frangipane talks about the struggle that some leaders have had in attempting to mobilize their churches for advancement in their city: "Many pastors, upon entering the ministry, heard the Lord whisper to their inner man, I have given you this city."[1] Yet in their attempt to advance the church, another voice arose and stopped their forward progress. Frangipane speaks of the challenge that confronted David when he went up to take Jerusalem. He had to overcome the Jebusites. The Jebusites were the fiercest of Israel's opponents and the last of the enemies that Israel had to overcome to take the Promised Land.

Frangipane goes on to say, "Many of Israel's greatest heroes attempted to conquer the Jebusites, but no one from Joshua to the Judges had succeeded. Thus the Jebusites were contemptuous when they heard of David's plan to possess their chief city, Jerusalem. They mocked Israel's young king: 'You shall not come in here, but the blind and lame shall turn you away.'" (2 Sam. 5:6)[2]

Because of woundedness, fear, division, lack of vision, and/or inability to see the need to advance, many in the church have held back advancement.[3] David is a model leader for this time in history. Nothing stopped David. He overcame the last enemies of God in Canaan. He was a bold apostolic leader. Neither the cries of the wounded nor those with lack of vision kept him from taking Jerusalem. He advanced because God told him to do so. The Breaker was going before him to break open the way.

The New Generation Is Radical

There is a generation in the church who can feel something radical stirring inside of them. They are sick of a maintenance-oriented, me-centered, watered-down, sin-friendly gospel. They have read the Bible and the passion of the apostolic leaders of the New Testament church burns inside of them. They want to see what happened in Scripture happen today. These people are neither religious nor traditional, and they are longing for a real fight.

They do not see the Jesus of the Gospels as a society-endorsing, religious-handshaking, racially-unjust, and Jezebel-tolerating God. They are not tolerant of that which is an enemy of God. Their gospel confronts the sin and demons that hold souls captive. It also confronts that which holds an entire group or society captive.

Their God Is Not Meek and Mild

Their God is one who shakes up, moves out, and changes individuals and groups. Their God is one who can change a nation, leading the church of Jesus Christ out of a captive state and into an advancing, invading force. Their God is the same God who led Israel out of Egypt and into the Promised Land, not to come into agreement with the Canaanites, but to utterly cut off the enemy and take their possessions (see Exod. 23:23). Their God is described in Micah 2:13: "The breaker goes up before them; they break out, pass through the gate, and go out by it. So their king goes on before them, and the LORD at their head" (NAS).

This is a gate-crashing, wall-breaking, and obstacle-removing God. In Colossians 2, Paul said in verse 10, "and you are complete in Him, who is the head of all principality and power." Then in verse 15 he said, "Having disarmed principalities and powers, He made a public spectacle of them, triumphing over them in it." God is the originator of every power and principality as well as the Victor over them through Jesus' death and resurrection.

The Breaker Is One
Who Breaks Open the Way

Micah 2:13 says, "The one who breaks open will come up before them; they will break out, pass through the gate, and go out by it; their king will pass before them, with the LORD at their head." In other words, there is no "way" that is impenetrable to God. Any way or route, which He has ordained for us to go through, He will break it open even if it seems blocked. God the Breaker goes up before us. This is not an ordinary person on our side. It is the King who will pass through before us. In Old Testament times invading forces used battering rams to break through gates (see Ezek. 21:22). Because God is at the head and is up front, He is the battering ram who butts open the way.

The term "breaker" is foreign to most Christians. *Barnes' Notes* says that the "Breaker-Through" was one of the titles given to Christ. The image here in Micah is one both of conquering and deliverance. (*Barnes' Notes* limits it to deliverance.) Something has to be broken through. Something has to be overcome. This breakthrough crashes a gate in order to move them into the open place. It is a place where they are not confined as in a prison. The gate of the prison (that which was holding them back) was burst open, to set them free. This is the same image found in Isaiah 43:6 when God said through Isaiah; "I will say to the North, give up; and to the South, Hold not back."[4]

Breakthrough is something that we cannot do by ourselves. It requires divine intervention. God has given apostolic people territories to take and adversity to overcome which they cannot do by themselves. We need God to break through for us. In the same way God led Moses and broke open the way in those days in how He is leading the church today.

Scriptural Examples of Breakthrough

God said to Moses, "I will do it." He is saying that to us also. What God meant is that Moses was to go ahead and take action. At the right time, God would release His intervention and power. Though God said He would do it, Moses had to believe God and initiate bold action. He had to go before Pharaoh and confront him. Yet God is the One who broke through for them. But Moses' faith, expressed through his action, released God to act. A mighty breakthrough occurred when through Moses, God visibly led Israel out of Egypt.

"Depart! Depart! Go out from there, touch no unclean thing; go out from the midst of her, be clean, you who bear the vessels of the LORD. For you shall not go out with haste, nor go by flight; for the LORD will go before you, and the God of Israel will be your rear guard" (Isa. 52:11-12). Hosea spoke of a breakthrough for Israel in Hosea 1:11, "Then the children of Judah and the children of Israel shall be gathered together, and appoint for themselves one head; and they shall come up out of the land, for great will be the day of Jezreel!" This is speaking of Israel breaking out of captivity into a free, open place; the land God was giving them. Jezreel means "God sows." Simultaneously God began to plant for them a great harvest.

Breakthrough occurred when Israel was released from captivity in Babylon and returned home to rebuild the temple in Jerusalem and reestablish their land (see Isa. 48:20). They had to break through forces exerted through people like Sanballat and Tobiah who did not want them to repossess what had been theirs. These are days that God is raising up a people who will reclaim lost land and inheritances, both naturally and spiritually. In doing so we will face an enemy who does not want us to have what is rightfully ours, but the Breaker is going before us to give us what is our destined heritage.

In another passage in Isaiah we can see the spiritual meaning of deliverance from prison brought out through the work of our coming Redeemer, Christ. Isaiah 42:6-7 says, "I, the LORD, have called You in righteousness, and will hold Your hand; I will keep You and give You as a covenant to the people, as a light to the Gentiles, to open blind eyes, to bring out prisoners from the prison, those who sit in darkness from the prison house." This same thought is carried over into Isaiah 61:1, "The Spirit of the Lord GOD is upon Me, because the LORD has anointed Me . . . to proclaim liberty to the captives, and the opening of the prison to those who are bound."

C.F. Keil and Franz Delitzsch, in their commentary on the Old Testament, wrote about God the Breaker.[5] The redemption of Israel from exile was likened to being liberated from captivity. Egypt was a slave house just as a prison with walls and gates. Both must be broken through in order to find freedom and obtain one's inheritance. While in captivity, it is locked up and access to it is denied.

The authors went on to say that it was the Breaker that went before Israel through a human leader responding to God. Led by Him, the people broke through walls; they marched through the gate and went through it out of prison. These three actions, break through, march through, and go out, describe an advancement which could not be stopped by any human power. King Jehovah was at their head. Just as He went before them in the wilderness, He will go before us now and lead the procession into breaking through to break out. This is a picture of a bold, courageous, believing, and victorious people who absolutely trust God and His leadership. There are two specifics characteristics of God the Breaker. They are:

1. The Breaker is a King with Kingdom authority.

This One is both King and Lord. A king is one who reigns or rules. He has sovereign power over a designated kingdom. From the beginning of time, all things created in heaven and earth have come from God including thrones and kingdoms. Colossians 1:16 says, "For by Him all things were created that are in heaven and that are on earth, visible and invisible, whether thrones or dominions or principalities or powers. All things were created through Him and for Him." This Breaker has all authority to enter into every other kingdom and nation and begin to break us out of those kingdoms' rule into a place of freedom and liberty, life and inheritance. He not only breaks us out of the imprisoning kingdom but also establishes a new Kingdom in its stead. He is *the* King of kings.

2. The Breaker is a covenant-maker and a covenant-keeper.

God is Jehovah in the Hebrew, meaning the Covenant-Keeper. This One who goes before us is both reigning over the kingdoms of heaven and earth, as well as making a covenant with us. Deuteronomy 28 is the classic covenant chapter in the Old Testament where God outlines what He has covenanted to do for those who will listen to Him, obey His Word, and be a believing people filled with faith. The Bible is comprised of the Old and New Testament. Another word for testament is covenant. Therefore, the Bible is also the Old and New Covenant. It is the written agreement of God on our behalf. God as Jehovah is at the head. He is the God whose word is true. He is not a liar.

Hebrews 6:17-20 says, "Thus God, determining to show more abundantly to the heirs of promise the immutability (unchangeableness) of His counsel, confirmed it by an oath, that by two immutable things, in which it is impossible for God to lie, we might have strong consolation, who have fled for refuge to lay hold of the hope set before us. This hope we have as an anchor of the soul, both sure and steadfast, and which enters the Presence behind the veil, where the forerunner has entered for us, even Jesus, having become High Priest forever according to the order of Melchizedek."

The author of Hebrews writes this verse following a statement about the promise God made to Abraham. A covenant is also a promise. Our expectation, framed by this covenant, causes us to press into God, enter His presence, receive the assurance we need to arise, and then act, knowing God will go before us and open up the way.

The Core Anointing of the Apostolic Church

These are days when God is calling the church into incomprehensibly large vision. The church is the body of Christ, which on earth will possess the kingdoms of this world as co-laborers and joint-heirs with Christ who is the Head. This is not a milk toast vision of the church. We need a revelation of God the Breaker to possess that which is before us. I believe the most critical manifestation of God necessary in the apostolic (New Reformation) church for advancement is that of God as the Breaker. In fact the breaker anointing is the core anointing of the apostolic church for advancement.

Notes

[1] Francis Frangipane, *The River of Life*, (Cedar Rapids, Iowa: Advancing Church Publications, 1993) p. 48.
[2] Ibid.
[3] Ibid, p. 44.
[4] Albert Barnes, *Barnes' Notes* (Seattle, WA: PC Bible Study, BibleSoft, 1998), Micah 2:13.
[5] C.F. Keil and Franz Delitzsch, *Keil and Delitzsch Commentary on the Old Testament,* (Seattle, WA: PC Bible Study, BibleSoft, 1998) Micah 2:13.

CHAPTER FOUR:

BREAKING THROUGH
AND BREAKING OUT

The first sentence of Micah 2:13 says: "The breaker goes up before them; they break out, pass through the gate, and go out by it." We are talking about the Breaker and breaking through. What does it mean to break through?

The Definition of Break Out

The Hebrew word for "break out" found in this chapter is *parats*. It means to break out, to burst out, to grow, to increase, to be opened. The implication is that something has been closed off, shut up, diminished, stunted, restricted, or confined. It is eye opening to realize how many different aspects of spiritual life are associated with the Breaker. *Parats* has to do with breaking out of a prison-like structure, growing in something, increasing in any area, and opening that which has been shut up.

Synonyms for "break" include to shatter, smash, break up, crush, splinter, burst, break in pieces, demolish, or eradicate. These are manifestations that are both spiritual and natural. In other words something is broken through in the spiritual realm and it manifests in the physical realm or sense realm. We can see it, experience it, feel it, or hear it.

An example of this is something that happened recently when I was speaking at a prophetic conference. While the musicians were playing after I spoke, I had a vision. In the vision I saw a glass ceiling. The people beneath the ceiling could see through the glass to where they needed to go, they were unable to penetrate the ceiling. They had vision because they could see where they were supposed to head. However the glass represented a wall that had been raised up against them to keep them from moving into God's place for them.

Suddenly the glass began to shatter and I could see and hear the pieces of glass "chink" as they hit the floor. The glass ceiling was shattering. That was a spiritual vision, a picture of what God was doing right then. As the vision came to an end, one of the singers began breaking forth into a new song that had never been sung before. As the song rang out, a great spirit of revelation began to break out on those that were at the meeting. That which had been obstructing their forward progress was removed.

The Scriptural Manifestations of "*Parats*": Release of Revelation

In 1 Samuel 3:1 there is an example of breaking through. This passage is about the transition from an old system to a new one, or an old move to a new one. Because of compromise on Eli's part, revelation was shut up. The second part of verse 1 says: "And the word of the LORD was precious in those days; there was no open vision." (KJV) The New King James says, "there was no widespread revelation." The Hebrew word for open or widespread is *parats*, the same word for break out. The implication is that something has to be broken through for revelation to be released. But here in 1 Samuel, there was no breakthrough revelation. There was no revelation that was breaking them out of where they were. They were stuck.

Sometimes the thing that is holding us back is the failure to perceive spiritually. We have no revelation. One of the words for hardness of heart in the Greek is *sklerokardia*, meaning destitute of spiritual perception. There is a natural-mindedness that needs to be broken through for revelation to be released. Without that breakthrough, our minds are darkened. There is a veil that blinds every Christian who fails to seek the Lord until revelation breaks through.

This is also true of those who have not been born again. In 2 Corinthians 4:3-4 the Word says that the gospel is veiled to those who are perishing, "whose minds the god of this age has blinded, who do not believe, lest the light of the gospel of the glory of Christ, who is the image of God, should shine on them."

Things Which Restrict Breakthrough in Revelation

Just as in the vision of the glass ceiling breaking, and then immediate revelation being poured out, revelation requires breakthrough. Whatever it may be that restricts the revelatory unfolding of truth from God to us has to be broken through. Paul says there is a veil that has to be broken through. Sometimes it is not natural-mindedness but sin that darkens our understanding and causes spiritual blindness. When sin is confessed and turned from, revelation that produces vision and direction can break through

At other times the enemy withholds or closes off revelation from us as in the case of Daniel. Daniel had to persist in prayer and fasting for 21 days to break the hold of the enemy from the revelation he needed. Then it took Michael, one of the chief angelic princes, to overcome the Prince of Persia. When that happened, revelation about the latter times was released to Daniel. In other words, there was a breakthrough revelation. An obstruction was broken up so that truth could break through.

In February, 2000 a high-level prayer team led by Chuck Pierce went around the world, stopping at several key cities interceding over two issues: the emergence of the apostolic leadership for the church around the world and the release of wealth to the church. Our church's intercessory teams backed them here in the United States. While they were in Singapore, the last city on their itinerary, I knew that they had broken through. The reason I knew was because I awakened to the revelatory voice of God speaking to me. When break through occurs, the voice of God is released. Another way to say it is that the heavens open. Revelation is released.

This is what I heard the Lord say in my spirit: "I am making My true apostolic leaders to be like Moses. No longer will the weaknesses in My leadership cause shame throughout the land. No longer will their gifts remain in isolation. Their weaknesses will now become strengths and cause them to become a battering ram. I will take this battering ram and pursue the Pharaoh system from territory to territory until the structure is shattered and dismantled. This will bring a visitation of death upon what has withstood My purposes throughout the nations of the earth. I am raising up an army that will usher in My glory. These are days of visitation and realignment, but this will be done through confrontation. Do not fear confrontation, for it shall not alienate but realign My purposes for victory. I am about to dismantle the occult structure that has kept My apostolic strength from coming forth."

To Break Forth Is to Expand

Isaiah 54:3 translates the word *parats* as break forth or expand. In the New King James version it says, "For you shall expand to the right and to the left, and your descendants will inherit the nations, and make the desolate cities inhabited." It means to break forth, break out, and burst out on the right and on the left. This is a day of breaking out into increase and enlargement. This is a day of breaking into the inheritance that is ours. But there is a breaking out of old mindsets and blindness that must happen to break into the revelation of what is to be ours in this season.[1]

For some it is breaking out of barrenness. There is an anointing being released right now for those whose physical, familial, financial, creative, emotional, and/or spiritual wombs have been shut up. This is also the day of the harvest and the turning of cities. The mistake many make is to wait until they *feel* like the promise is true. We must learn to differentiate between how we feel about something versus what God says. God will bring our desires and feelings into alignment with His when we begin to act on what God says. Feelings always follow faith and faith is manifested in action.

The Relationship of
Faith to Breaking Out

Years ago while in college, I learned a simple formula from an InterVarsity staff person. Faith is first. Facts are second and will line up with faith. Feelings are third and are a result of faith affecting facts that change the way we feel. Most of us get the order wrong and determine our faith by our feelings. In fact some even change their theology to line up with experience rather than the Word of God. So their faith begins to be based not on the Word of God, but on their experiences. Consequently they do not get scriptural results because their belief structure is not based on faith, but on sight.

To Spread Abroad: Breaking Out
of Geographical Constraints

Parats is also translated as spread abroad, as we see in Genesis 28:14: "Also your descendants shall be as the dust of the earth; you shall spread abroad to the west and the east, to the north and the south; and in you and in your seed all the families of the earth shall be blessed." The implication here is that no matter what the obstacles to increase are, because God has said it, there will be a breaking through every hindrance and bursting out of any type of isolating, diminishing factor. There are geographical implications for break out. It is not just to increase in number but also to spread into more and more territories, breaking into places previously untouched by the gospel.

Because of our spiritual DNA which God has deposited into us, Christians should be boundary-breakers. We are to break out of a confined territory and enter into ever increasing boundaries in every area of our lives. This goes back to the original apostolic mandate of multiplying and filling the earth in Genesis 1:28. If we are to fill the earth then we must reproduce and move into new geographic boundaries, expanding our borders. Psalm 18:19 says, "He brought me forth also into a large place; he delivered me, because he delighted in me" (KJV).

Filling the earth was the mindset of apostolic leaders in the New Testament. Paul was constantly planning and pursuing new missionary (apostolic) journeys. He was constantly extending the borders of the territories that had received the gospel. More than any other apostle in that day, Paul began to fill the earth with the gospel. He broke out of the confines of the local church at Antioch and broke into geographic territories where the gospel had never been heard. Paul's overarching passion was to reach the ends of the earth.

The Power of the Holy Spirit to Break Us Out Territorially

In Acts 1:8 we are told the purpose for the baptism in the Holy Spirit: "But you shall receive power when the Holy Spirit has come upon you; and you shall be witnesses to Me in Jerusalem, and in all Judea and Samaria, and to the end of the earth." So many in the church say, "I got it." But we don't have an "it," we have a living person residing in us by the power of the Holy Spirit. Jesus Himself has taken up residence within our spirits. He comes to empower and enable us to be and do everything we have been destined to be and do.

The empowering of the Holy Spirit is not just about speaking in another language unknown to us. It is about an empowering by God Himself to break out of the confines of our current borders and to be witnesses even to the end of the earth. We are to break into previously closed areas, taking the gospel into every geographic area of the earth. That takes the "breaker anointing." Apostolic people are, therefore, to be a "breaker people."

Breaking Through Is Overcoming the Enemies of God

Breakthrough is also related to overcoming the enemies of God. Second Samuel 5 is the story of David taking on the Philistines. We know from Judges 3 that one of the enemies of Israel left in Canaan was the Philistines. They were left there to both teach the Israelites how to war as well as to test the Israelites in their obedience to God (see Judges 3:1-4).

The Lord had instructed David to go up against the Philistines. David obeyed the Lord and, as a result, the Philistines were defeated. In 2 Samuel 5:20 of *The Living Bible* is the account of the Philistines' defeat. "So David went out and fought with them at Baal-perazim and defeated them. 'The Lord did it!' he exclaimed. 'He burst through my enemies like a raging flood.' So he named the place 'Bursting.'" Baal-perazim means "the master of breakthrough." God manifested Himself through David as the Master of Breakthrough. He burst forth from David and his army through to the Philistines like water breaks through a dam. That is literally what it means, the breaking through of dammed up water.

Imagine the force of the water in Hoover Dam if some power were to break the dam. That is the image of breakthrough here in 2 Samuel 5. When God goes forth as the

Breaker, it is as if a dam of water has broken loose against its restraints. It not only destroys but also sweeps away the enemy. All of the articles belonging to the enemy army are carried away also. This is a powerful picture of breakthrough.

Our Destiny Is to Break Out of Every Enslaving Situation

Even in the midst of slavery and its accompanying oppression, there was a breaker anointing on the Israelites. Exodus 1:12 says, "the more they afflicted them, the more they multiplied and grew." They were in dread of the children of Israel. There is a destiny of increase on God's people. It is only our faith and obedience that limits the increase. The word here in Exodus 1 for grew is, once again, *parats*, or break out. In the midst of deep trouble, in which they were slaves to the Egyptians, the children of Israel broke forth in their population. Nothing could hinder the seed of destiny that God had implanted in them. Within that seed was a break out anointing. Not even slavery and bondage could stop that which had been planted deep within their spiritual DNA. So it is today. We have that same DNA within us.

Breakthrough Brings Us into Increase and Wealth

The Old Testament patriarchs expected an inheritance and increase. From the very first man and woman on earth, God spoke this as part of their destiny. To achieve such increase takes breakthrough. Breakthrough not only pertains to our descendants but to our possessions. In Genesis 30:29-30, breakthrough and break out pertains to wealth. Jacob was working for his father-in-law, Laban, and said to him, "You know how I have served you and how your livestock has been with me. For what you had before I came was little, and it is now increased to a great amount; the LORD has blessed you since my coming. And now, when shall I also provide for my own house?" The word for increased in that verse means broken out.

The word *parats* occurs in a parallel Scripture about wealth, prosperity, and financial increase. Proverbs 3:9-10 says, "Honor the LORD with your possessions, and with the firstfruits of all your increase; So your barns will be filled with plenty, and your vats will overflow with new wine." The overflowing vats means vats that will "burst out" with new wine. Notice that breakthrough is linked with giving here. There is a breaking out, a bursting out that will occur when we honor God with giving according to His Word.

One of the marks of an apostolic people and apostles is that money follows them. Money is not an issue for an apostle. In Acts they laid money at the apostles' feet. Giving flowed and it released a breakthrough. Some of the greatest breakthroughs I have personally witnessed have been at meetings where there was abandoned, abundant giving which was instigated by the Holy Spirit.

The breaker anointing releases increase that includes wealth and finances. Something must be broken through in order to reach a place of enlargement. Here Jacob brought breakthrough to Laban. The blessing of the Lord is to be on us as God's own people. Proverbs 10:22 says, "The blessing of the LORD brings wealth, and he adds no trouble to it." (NIV)

Wealth is more than money. It is abundance and relates to anything that is in abundance. It can be an abundance of ideas, contents, property, or products. It is a large amount of something. Prosperity also means more than physical wealth and is a result of increase. The Apostle John said "Beloved, I pray that you may prosper in all things and be in health, just as your soul prospers" (3 John 1:2) The word prosper means to succeed in reaching, to succeed in business affairs, to make progress. It also means to succeed, flourish, thrive, and to grow. It is connected to favor. This cannot happen without breakthrough.

Become Spiritually-Minded

We are to break out of small-mindedness, old mindsets, and our own human thinking into the mind and plans of God. Paul said in 1 Corinthians 2:9-11 "Eye has not seen, nor ear heard, nor have entered into the heart of man the things which God has prepared for those who love Him. But God has revealed them to us through His Spirit. For the Spirit searches all things, yes, the deep things of God. For what man knows the things of a man except the spirit of the man which is in him? Even so no one knows the things of God except the Spirit of God."

Paul went on to say that if we try to figure out the things of God with our natural minds, we would not understand or perceive them. Why? Because in 1 Corinthians 2:14 he said, "the natural man does not receive the things of the Spirit of God, for they are foolishness to him; nor can he know them, because they are spiritually discerned." That is why so many fail to comprehend the full purposes of God; because they limit their experience and destiny to what they can figure out with their natural minds.

God has put within us His Holy Spirit. His presence within us is God in us. Part of the identity of God is as the Breaker.

Every single person filled with the Holy Spirit is filled with the Breaker and has access to this anointing. In the Breaker is the ability to break through every wall, every hindrance, and every obstacle.

Notes
[1] The book *Possessing Your Inheritance* (Renew Books) by Chuck D. Pierce and Rebecca Wagner Sytsema is an excellent resource for further understanding on the topic of breaking into one's inheritance.

CHAPTER FIVE:

BREAKTHROUGH AT THE GATES

M icah 2:13 says the people who were behind a gate in a tight, confined area broke out; they passed through the gate. Why? Because the Breaker had gone before them and used His authority and force to open the gates that had been closed.

The Holy Spirit never made a mistake when He inspired the writing of Scripture. Specific words were used because of the meaning that they held in that day. The word "gates" was used for a specific reason. They are linked with many things in Scripture, some of which are important for us to understand as we study the breaker anointing.

What Are Gates?

Gates represent many things in Scripture. Everything they

represent requires a manifestation of God as the Breaker in order to break through into all of the dimensions represented. However it is not the intent here to deal with the whole meaning of gates but to focus on them as entry and exit points that must be opened in order to enter or exit. The other focus of this chapter relative to gates is their structure. Knowledge of the structure of the gates in Old Testament times releases revelation and understanding concerning the full challenge we face in breaking through.

The Church is the Gate of Heaven

In Genesis 28:17 God revealed something about gates to Jacob that we have begun to understand in a new way in the past three or four years. Jacob "was afraid and said, 'How awesome is this place! This is none other than the house of God, and this is the gate of heaven!'" The church is the house of God in the New Testament. The house of God is the place where the gate of heaven resides. When the gate opens it either lets what is on earth ascend through the gates into heaven, or it lets what is in heaven descend into the earth. It is through these gates that heaven comes down to earth.

When Jesus' disciples came and asked Him how to pray, He told the disciples to pray in this manner. Part of the way Jesus instructed the disciples to pray is that God's will be done on earth as it is in heaven and that His Kingdom come on earth as it is in heaven. For heaven to come on earth would require real breakthrough. God is looking for a people who believe this and will release heaven on earth by breaking through.

We know from Micah 2:13 that God the Breaker goes before us and breaks open the way. Something compels God into action to open those gates. That compelling force is faith coupled with obedience. I do not want to go into a discussion of those two elements here but true faith is powerful. It opens the gate of heaven. When heaven's gates open, what is in heaven comes down to earth. Health, wholeness, peace, love, grace, glory, revelation, strategy, and all the rest of the nature of God and His Kingdom come down when the gates open.

Years ago I made a hospital visit to pray for a girl who had leukemia. I personally observed the sores in her mouth caused by the chemotherapy. She was unable to eat and was on intravenous feedings. She also had a huge very deep sore on her knee that was so inflamed she could not walk. I cannot remember now all of the details, but what I do remember is that I prayed for her ability to eat and for God to heal her mouth as well as her knee. That night I got a call and she was up walking around eating Fritos. That was a breakthrough! The gates of heaven opened and healing was released on earth through the power of the Holy Spirit.

The Structure and Purpose of Old Testament Gates

Understanding the structure of gates in the Old Testament helps us understand what was involved when Scripture talks about gates. Gates then were much different than a wire fence with a swinging gate and a simple latch. They were entryways into or out of cities. Every city was walled. Gates were constructed within the wall to allow people to enter and exit. On top of the gates was an area where the watchmen stood to watch who was coming to enter the city as well as who was leaving. The watchmen would send information down to the gatekeepers to say, "let this one in, keep this one out." They also informed the gatekeepers of approaching enemies.

The purpose of the walls and gates was to protect the city, the inhabitants, and their possessions. They kept certain people out of the city. At night the gates were shut to prevent marauders or bandits, other undesirables or wild animals from entering at will. It was also through the gates that supplies came in and went out. Whatever or whoever came in or out of a city had to do so through the gates. There was no other way in or out. Both good and evil came in or left a city through the gates.

The structure of walls and gates was much different from today. Both the walls and gates were several feet thick. Some gates were on a pulley-like apparatus that allowed them to be raised or lowered. They did not open like a contemporary door swings open. They were raised or lowered. It is this type of gate that is being referred to in Psalm 24:7: "Lift up your heads, O you gates! And be lifted up, you everlasting doors! And the King of glory shall come in." There were also gates which swung open and closed as a door does today.

Isaiah 45:2 is another reference to breaking through gates. "I will go before you and make the crooked places straight; I will break in pieces the gates of bronze (brass) and cut the bars of iron." The gates being referred to here were the gates of Babylon. Babylon had 100 massive gates, 25 on each of the four sides of the city. They were made of brass.[1] These were gates that swung open and closed as a door does.

Without God the Breaker, the Gates Will Not Open

God was saying to Cyrus the King, "I will go before you. I will prepare the way for conquest. I will demonstrate the fact that it is I who has empowered you to triumph. The ability to break in pieces the gates of brass is so beyond your ability that when they break open, everyone will know that it is I who have gone before you to do it. I will take away everything that would prevent you from achieving victory in this conquest." That is basically what is being said here. It sounds like a parallel Scripture to Micah 2:13.

Barnes' Notes says about the gates of iron in Isaiah 45:2: "One method of securing the gates of fortified places among the ancients, was to cover them with thick plates of iron— a custom which is still used in the East."[2]

The details written in Isaiah 45:2 are important to emphasize because it helps us understand that without God intervening, these gates would never break open. The structure of these gates was such that it would be impossible for a human being to break through them. Supernatural intervention from the Breaker was required. God, therefore, victoriously went before them and broke through. The same is true today. We need the supernatural intervention of God to break through impenetrable gates in order to enter into new territories and new places.

The Meaning of Threshold: Its Implication in Warfare

There were also thresholds. It seems from Scripture that there were thresholds within the gates particularly to the Temple. There are two words for threshold in the Hebrew. These words reveal that there is warfare at the gates, and that there is warfare over the threshold.

One of the Hebrew words is *caph*.[3] It is the word used for door (post), gate, post, and threshold. *Caph* is from *caphaph* a primitive root that means to snatch away or terminate. The second word used for threshold in the Hebrew is *miphtan* that is from *pethen* an unused root meaning to twist as a snake. It is pronounced much like python and is probably where the name of the snake was derived from.[4] Pythons destroy their prey by wrapping their bodies around them and suffocating them.

Fear and Death Oppose Our Forward Movement

Basically there are two principalities that oppose our moving forward when it comes to breaking through. One is a principality that rules through fear. It attempts to terminate our forward movement by snatching us away. When someone is threatened with being snatched away, fear is induced. So one of the structures we face at the threshold results in fear. Realize that just as this demonic structure is there to snatch us away, God is also present to snatch us out of the hand of the enemy and take us through the gate across to the other side. Psalm 91:3 says, "Surely He shall deliver you from the snare of the fowler."

The second principality that opposes our moving forward is a python-like demonic structure that attempts to squeeze the life out of us. We feel as if we are going to die.

It is at the threshold where we have to overcome. It tries to take away our breath that sustains life. However, God is there to breathe prophetic breath into us which is life-imparting. There is always a crisis over the prophetic word at the gate. If we hear the word, we know how to proceed. If we do not, we are lost and do not have the infusion of life and hope to break through.

Breath and the Prophetic Word

One structure (fear) attempts to terminate our forward progress. The other structure (the python-like spirit) is a life-crushing force that takes away our breath. Often breath is referred to as the prophetic wind or word. The nature of the prophetic wind referred to in Ezekiel 37 is that it is a life-giving force. Therefore, the python-like structure directly opposes the prophetic in order to leave us directionless and lifeless. We lack vision and do not know how to go forward. We feel surrounded by a sense of spiritual darkness or blindness. We have lost our way and it seems like we are about to die; like our lights have been punched out. Hope is lost and despair settles upon us like a wet blanket, suffocating and sickening. Forward progress is temporarily halted.

That is why it is so important not to squelch the prophetic ministry and wind of God. Prophetic revelation will pump life and vision into us enabling us to overcome the warfare at the threshold. So many times I have watched a person or ministry hindered by opposition. It has siphoned off every bit of life and courage they have to boldly move forward. Then along comes someone with the prophetic word from God for their situation. That word or revelation imparts faith, life, and liberty. Where they were scraping the bottom of the barrel, suddenly they feel buoyed up by supernatural impartation from God. This is an expression of the Breaker.

The Threshold:
A Concentration of Demonic Forces

Almost always when we are being led into new territory or new exploits, there is warfare at the threshold. In fact this is the place of the greatest concentration of demonic forces arising to halt our crossing over. They oppose forward progress. We see this dynamic when Peter and John broke through to the miracle at the Gate Beautiful.

The authorities responded by saying in Acts 4:17 "But so that it spreads no further among the people, let us severely threaten them, that from now on they speak to no man in this name." They opposed the forward movement propelled by breakthrough. Peter and John broke through a threshold.

Think about the meaning of the word threshold. The threshold is where something kicks into action. It is the minimal amount of something needed to induce a corresponding action. For instance, we refer to the threshold of pain, threshold of new discovery, or threshold of a door. It is the point of entry into the next place or experience. Consider the pain threshold. When the minimal amount of stimuli required to cause our receptors to register pain is reached, we feel pain. Even if the receptors are being stimulated prior to the feeling of pain, a certain amount is required before it registers in our consciousness. The threshold is the point at which change registers.

The Threshold Is the Brink Where Fear Is Experienced

Threshold also means brink. We have to go to the brink if we are to move into the new territory or place. Every brink has a drop off, a chasm, and a precipice. If we go any farther, we will fall off the edge and all will be lost.

I remember riding up to the top of Mount Washington in New Hampshire. My husband was driving. I sat in the front right passenger seat and looked out over the side of the mountain. The route to the top took us around the outside of the mountain. There were no guardrails to keep us from going over the edge if for any reason the car lost control. I became aware of what a precipice was and the feeling was overwhelming. In all my courage I remember finally climbing down in the well of the car in the right front and yelling to my husband, "Quit laughing and tell me when we get to the top." I hated riding the precipice. I felt death was imminent.

There was great fear at the precipice of the mountain. When we arrived at the top, inside the building was a sign telling how many people had died when their car brakes failed and they tumbled over the edge. That fueled my fear even more. Going down the mountain I immediately crawled back into the well of the car. The greatest fear we face is at the threshold.

The Threshold Is a Place of Risk

The threshold represents the place of risking total loss. It is the place of greatest vulnerability. Yet it is also the place from which we must leap if we are to get to the other side. It is the place where faith must arise. Without faith we will not make it to the other side. It is the place of risk. Either we hold on to everything and clutch what is secure, or we let go and leap. When we leap, will God be there to catch us and carry us to the other side?

In Exodus 19:4 it is just this sense that God expressed to the Israelites. In facing their threshold or brink, which was marching through the gates out of Egypt, Israel had to make a leap of faith. When they took the leap of faith, would God come and bear them up on eagle's wings? God said, "You have seen what I did to the Egyptians, and how I bore you on eagles' wings and brought you to Myself." God did come through for Israel and opened up the Red Sea. He swooped down and picked them up, carrying them on His wings. However, they had to leap first. Had they not taken bold daring action, which is faith, God could not have come and saved them.

Bold Action at the Threshold Is Required to Open Gates

Something that has become obvious is that bold action has faith attached to it. The action can be good or evil. Faith-filled people take bold action. That action opens a gate and releases spiritual power. If the bold action is evil, it opens an evil gate. For instance, when the first school student in the United States shot and killed fellow students and/or teachers, that action opened a gate. It was a type of faith, albeit evil in nature. That student believed something that caused him to take that specific evil action. As a result, school shootings are common today because an evil gate was opened.

Paul opened up a righteous gate in Ephesus when he boldly preached the gospel there in the city. Not only were people changed but the socioeconomic system of the city was changed. City transformation occurred (see Acts 19).

Apostles, as well as apostolic people, are called to live on the cutting edge. They are pioneers forging a new way. The cutting edge is the direction given by the prophetic word of God that releases breakthrough and, therefore, the presence of God into a church or city in a powerful way. They are called to bold, daring, fear-overcoming, breathtaking, and impossible actions in order to accomplish the vision God has given to them. That bold action opens up a gate of spiritual power and blessing from God. The heavens over an area are opened in a new way. If the vision is attainable in their strength and power, it is not from God. In fact, the vision that God gives to apostles and apostolic people brings them to the threshold again and again. It is at the gates, when one enters the threshold, that faith and perseverance are tested. It is at the threshold where either spiritual abortion or spiritual birthing occurs.

Faith and Perseverance Are Needed

God has a great deal for us to possess, but it will take great faith and perseverance. God is continually putting new conquests before us to develop our faith and perseverance at a higher level. We must continually remind ourselves of what God instructed the Israelites in Judges 3:1-4. He said: "Now these are the nations which the LORD left, that He might test Israel by them, that is, all who had not known any of the wars in Canaan (this was only so that the generations of the children of Israel might be taught to know war, at least those who had not formerly known it), namely, five lords of the Philistines, all the Canaanites, the Sidonians, and the Hivites who dwelt in Mount Lebanon, from Mount Baal Hermon to the entrance of Hamath. And they were left, that He might test Israel by them, to know whether they would obey the commandments of the LORD, which He had commanded their fathers by the hand of Moses."

We can also decide we want to quit at some point because a gate seems too hard or too unconquerable. We may be tired and weary of the battle. We want to sit down, take a rest, and check out. We have the option of sitting down and living a life of ease. But by doing so we will never reach our potential because fear or weariness overtook us at the threshold. Some make this decision and fail to reach their destiny.

Paul said that he kept pressing on to attain that which he was intended to attain (see Phil. 3:12-14). God apprehended Paul not just to convert him but also to use Paul to accomplish a great ministry, to take the gospel to the Gentiles in many nations. Paul pressed through despite many trials.

Threshold Issues: Control, Hesitation, Abandonment, Faith

Control is an issue we must deal with at the threshold. Control has to be yielded at the threshold to make it to the other side. In other words, there is a risk we have to take, letting go of the known, and trusting God to get us across once we make the leap. It is as if we take our hands off the steering wheel of the car and let God take over.

Hesitation is another issue at the threshold. Hesitation is to be uncertain, indecisive, to waver, pause, or delay. Again, we hesitate because of fear. Fear will uncover what we serve in our heart. To what are we bowing down? Of what are we afraid? What will we lose? What we bow down to is what we worship. Is it God or is it something or someone else? Elijah challenged the people in 1 Kings 18:21 when he said to them, "How long will you halt between two opinions? Make your choice, choose between God or Baal." James exhorted the people to stop hesitating when he told them to have faith and not doubt. "Let him ask in faith, with no doubting, for he who doubts is like a wave of the sea driven and tossed by the wind" (James 1:5-6).

At the threshold Jesus' words begin to ring loud like the Liberty Bell in Philadelphia. In Mark 8:34-36 Jesus challenged the people: "When He had called the people to Himself, with His disciples also, He said to them, 'Whoever desires to come after Me, let him deny himself, and take up his cross, and follow Me. For whoever desires to save his life will lose it, but whoever loses his life for My sake and the gospel's will save it. For what will it profit a man if he gains the whole world, and loses his own soul?'" As the apostolic church arises, so will abandonment of self to God. On the horizon is a new consecration of the church to God.

It is here that our true abandonment to the will of God is tested. To take up the cross means that we will die to whatever is self-focused in order to attain that which is God initiated and directed. When we give up the right to ourselves, it is there we will find ourselves. We will find a new piece of who we really are.

At every threshold, when we give up our rights and future to God, losing ourselves, we find a new piece of our true life. True living is only that which fulfills the Father's will. Jesus said in John 4:34, "My food is to do the will of Him who sent Me, and to finish His work." Jesus went to the brink again and again. But in it He found Himself and He was nourished, He grew in strength and confidence in His Father.

Crossing over requires us to give up something that is precious to us such as a prized possession. It may be a thing, an attitude, a person, security, or our desires for our future. It can be anything that we hold on to when the only way to get to the other side is to let go of it. There is an aspect of idolatry to that. It has become a god to us, something we worship and to which we are bowing our knee. To cross over will mean to let go of that which will not fit through the gate with us.

Gates Are Where We Win or Lose

Gates are where we win or lose. That is why Scripture uses gates as the place to be broken through. We must break through intimidation, faithlessness, fear, hopelessness, despair, or whatever else looms like an unconquerable foe at the gates. The threshold is where we either leap forward or back out. Yet once we leap, it is where we meet the incredible supernatural power of God to break through before us victorious over every obstacle. It is after we leap that we begin to possess our inheritance for the current season. It is where increase and abundance come in whatever dimension we are crossing over into. It is there we meet God in a way that is new.

To refuse to leap is to make a choice to stop. We become stuck at that point. Before we can begin to increase again, we must return to the place where we made a choice to stop. However, once we can let go and leap, we will meet God in a completely new way. The new revelation of God will cause us to wonder why we were so hesitant. Yet without faith it is impossible to please God. So we will come to this place again and again and again.

The Gates of Hell Will Not Prevail

Jesus said to Peter that the church of Jesus Christ is being built on Himself, the rock and foundation of the church. He went on to say that the gates of hell would not prevail against, overpower, or overcome the church. In the Revised Standard Version it says that the powers of death will not overcome the church. At the threshold, it feels like we can lose everything. We feel as if we are going to die, at least figuratively if not literally. At the gates we may feel as if we will be overpowered and overcome. But in Matthew 16:18, the gates of the evil one, the gates of hell will not overtake us. Death will not do us in. In fact, it is there that at the gates that new resurrection power will be released. There will be a new wind of strength, victory, life, liberty, and joy released when we overcome at the gates.

The Breaker goes up before them; He breaks open the way!

Notes

[1] Robert Jamieson, A. R. Fausset, David Brown, *Jamieson-Fausset-Brown Bible Commentary*, (Seattle, WA: PC Bible Study, BibleSoft, 1998), notes on Isaiah 45:2.

[2] Albert Barnes, Barnes' Notes, (Seattle, WA: PC Bible Study, BibleSoft, 1998), notes on Micah 2:13.

[3] *Strong's Greek and Hebrew Dictionary*, (Seattle, WA: PC Bible Study, Bible Soft, 1998), *caph* (#5592); *caphaph* (#5605).

[4] Strong's Greek and Hebrew Dictionary, (Seattle, WA: PC Bible Study, Bible Soft, 1998), *miphtan* (#4670); *pethen* (#6620).

CHAPTER SIX:

CAUGHT IN
THE NARROW PLACE

Gates recur throughout our Christian walk. They are the places where we have to face the future in a new way. They are places of decision in which we decide to stay where we are or risk all and move forward. If we make a decision to stay where we are, we are actually making a decision to go backwards. It is at the gate that God gives us an opportunity to go backward.

Gates also represent places of crisis. The challenge delivering us to the door of a gate does not have to be a crisis. However we may move into crisis simply because of the way we respond. There is a conflict raging in our will. The debate over our will creates an internal crisis. If we do not recognize it and make a clear decision to arise and go forward, depression and despair will overtake us. Indecisiveness opens the door to negative emotions as well as to the enemy.

Captured By Emotions at the Gate

Often times when we are at the gate, we find ourselves in depression and do not understand why. We have not clearly understood the issues and so are overcome by emotions because of a vague feeling of uncertainty, dread, and hopelessness. This is part of the warfare at the gates. At the gate we face internal enemies, those from within ourselves, those we have inherited from previous generations (iniquities or weaknesses), and external enemies, those outside of ourselves. Pharaoh, Sanballat, and Tobiah are examples of external enemies. Pharaoh opposed Moses and the Israelites. Sanballat and Tobiah tried to stop Israel from rebuilding Jerusalem through fear.

At gates we become uncertain of the future and if we do not make a decision to move forward a blanket of despair will overtake us. Our past experiences feed our present response. If our experience has been one predominated by failure and loss, fear will arise like the giants of Canaan at the gates.

Despair and hopelessness will overtake us because we cannot get our bearings for our future. In fact we feel as if we have neither a future nor hope. A blanket of darkness will overwhelm us until we can begin to figure out what is going on and begin to take remedial action. We find ourselves in a crevice, a narrow place and do not know how to get out.

Understanding the Narrow Place

Scripture talks about the narrow place. Numbers 22:26 says that the "angel of the Lord went further, and stood in a narrow place, where was no way to turn either to the right hand or to the left." That is a picture of what it is like for us at the gate. It is a narrow place where we can either go forward or backward. But to go forward, we need the Breaker to come. Why? If God does not come as the Breaker, we will not make it through and will begin to go backwards.

There is a Scripture in 1 Samuel 13:5-6 which is a picture of our response when we get to gates. It says: "Then the Philistines gathered together to fight with Israel, thirty thousand chariots and six thousand horsemen, and people as the sand which is on the seashore in multitude. And they came up and encamped in Michmash, to the east of Beth Aven. When the men of Israel saw that they were in danger (for the people were distressed—in a narrow place), then the people hid in caves, in thickets, in rocks, in holes, and in pits." We may not hide in literal caves, thickets, and so forth. We will, however, find some place which we deem safe and go there. We tend to withdraw in some way or else we fight.

Defining the Narrow Place

The word for narrow is sometimes translated as trouble in the New Testament. Paul said in 2 Corinthians 4:8, "we are troubled on every side, yet not distressed; we are perplexed, but not in despair." In the New Testament it is also translated afflicted or to suffer tribulation. The word means pressure. Hebrews 11:37 says, "They were stoned, they were sawn asunder, were tempted, were slain with the sword: they wandered about in sheepskins and goatskins; being destitute, *afflicted*, tormented."

In the Old Testament, narrow is translated as a tight place, i.e. trouble; crowded by an opponent, adversary, afflicted, anguish, close, distress, enemy, foe, small, sorrow, strait, tribulation. Those words give a picture of extreme discomfort and challenge. That is why people feel as if the wind is knocked out of their sails at the gate. They feel overwhelmed or overcome in their emotions and their faith.

Depression is filled with hopelessness and despair. It denies the very truth of Scripture. God said through Jeremiah that He has come to give us a future and a hope (see Jer. 29:11). Even when Israel went into captivity in Egypt and in Babylon, God always arranged a way out. 2 Chronicles 15:4 talks about Israel: "When in their trouble they turned to the Lord God of Israel, and sought Him, He was found by them." Psalm 107:2 says: "Then they cried out to the Lord in their trouble, and He delivered them out of their distresses." Narrow is translated trouble and distress in these two passages. God found them and delivered them out of their narrow place.

Opportunity to Build a New History

It is at the gate that we have the opportunity to build a new history. Our history is that which we look back on as the story of our life. What our experience in the past has been is how we will tend to interpret our future. God instructed Israel to look back on their history and their experience and remember all the ways that God brought them out into a broad place through delivering them from their enemies. He even told them to rehearse their victories with their children. Their children needed to build a view of God in which they saw Him as the One who always caused them to triumph. The fathers were to do this by rehearsing all the ways God delivered them in the past.

I love the way the NIV expresses 2 Corinthians 2:14: "But thanks be to God, who always leads us in triumphal procession in Christ and through us spreads everywhere the fragrance of the knowledge of him." This expresses the sense of the King of kings going before us. And He went before the children of Israel.

If our history has been one of failure, defeat, or loss, we will struggle to believe at the gates. But it is at the gates that we can begin to build a new truth about our past. We can begin to make decisions that will release the presence and power of God into the situation changing our experience into success and victory.

When we face a gate, we are at a crossroad. Which fork we take will determine the harvest and inheritance we loose. Paul said that whatsoever a man sows, that will he reap (see Gal. 6:7). If we sow faith, we will reap the rewards of faith. We will obtain the promise. If we sow doubt and unbelief, we will reap the rewards by not entering the new place, the place of promise.

This was the plight of the Israelites who, through fear, were overcome by doubt and unbelief and failed to obtain their inheritance. It took a different generation to arise and go in and possess Canaan, the land of promise. It took a generation who was not overcome with fear, doubt, and unbelief.

Faith, Not Fear, Is the Key

Paul said to Timothy in 2 Timothy 1:7 that God had not given him a spirit of fear. Notice it is a spirit that releases fear. When fear comes, it is an evil spirit sent to undermine our faith. The word for fear there means timidity, dread, or faithlessness. To enter Canaan, it took a generation who refused to listen to a demon spirit that told them they could not go in. Faith is the key at the threshold. It is faith that moves God to action. Hebrews 11 is all about faith and what it accomplished.

Faith is what is needed at the gates. However there is a war over our faith. First Peter 5:8 says, "Be sober, be vigilant; because your adversary the devil walks about like a roaring lion, seeking whom he may devour." A roaring lion induces fear. We just noted that "God has not given us a spirit of fear, but of power and of love and of a sound mind" (2 Tim. 1:7). The enemy of our soul wants our full attention at the gate. Fear overtakes us so we will not move forward. Yet there is Another who is not like a roaring lion but is the Lion of the Tribe of Judah, the Mighty Warrior. He will fight for us and blast through every closed place.

How Faith Comes

Paul said in Romans 10:17 that faith comes by hearing and hearing by the word of God. The Greek term for "word" in this passage is *rhema*. *Rhema* is a personal word from God to us. *Rhema* occurs when we are reading Scripture and suddenly a verse goes right into our spirit. Or we may be hearing someone preach and they say something which goes to the core of our being. It is a personal word from the Lord to us through Scripture, the preached word, or in our prayer or worship time. What is needed is the prophetic voice or a *rhema* (a type of prophetic word) that will put us back on course and propel us forward through releasing faith.

Proverbs 29:18 says that without a vision, the people perish. If we study the original Hebrew in this passage, we see that it means that without prophetic impartation, we will lose heart, purpose and/or direction. The *Revised Standard Version* says: "where there is no prophecy, the people cast off restraint." The *Amplified Bible* says that where there is no vision or redemptive revelation of God, the people perish. Many people get lost in depression and believe they are victims of their past struggles. The real issue is they are in a battle and stuck at a gate or the narrow place. They are lodged in a crevice and there seems to be no way to become dislodged.

In California, a few years ago, a boy fell into a crevice between two mountains. He was stuck in this crevice that was very deep and he could not get out. No one could reach him. They called the rescue team to come. When the rescuers arrived, they had the right equipment to get him out. However, even with all their sophisticated equipment they could not get him.

The problem was that he was stuck in the crevice, a narrow place. The rescue operation continued for hours as they tried to pry him loose. Finally someone came up with the idea of getting some cooking oil and pouring it all over him. One member of the rescue team went to a local store and bought some bottles of cooking oil. He returned to the rescue operation and they poured the bottles of oil over the boy. They believed that when the boy was good and greased up, he would easily slip out of that narrow place. That was exactly what happened. As soon as they had poured oil over him, they were able to pull him right out. The resistance that was holding him in the narrow crevice was removed and he was able to break free.

Needed: A New Anointing

What people need is a new anointing. Like the oil that was poured over that boy, they need a new anointing that will cause them to slip through the narrow place. Remember the county fairs when they had the greased pig challenges where people tried to catch a greased pig? It's impossible because the pig just slips through their hands and arms. We need to be like greased pigs, smeared with the oil of God's anointing. No narrow place or demon spirit will be able to hold onto us.

We as believers need to press into God, dust our faith off, get into the Word of God and prayer, and begin to believe God for a fresh wind of prophetic revelation that will impart faith and vision. The Word of God is full of promise concerning our victory and our future. Everything in the Bible is about overcoming. That was, in part, what Jesus' death and resurrection were about. Jesus experienced the ultimate breakthrough when He overcame death. He had to risk dying to overcome it. The gates of hell or death could not prevail. If we cannot overcome, then the Word of God is a book of lies.

Everyone I know experiences a sense of the wind being knocked out of their sails when they are at a gate. The oppression at times is overwhelming. Some think they are in a major depression. The enemy's trap is to convince them of that fact. They are tempted to turn to counselors or drugs when what they need is to hear from God and then take decisive action. Instead they look back over their past and say, "look at all that happened to me negatively. Look at what God has promised me but has never happened." There is a war over the prophetic word of God at the gates.

Don't Let Your Past Determine Your Future

Many in the Bible had painful or traumatized pasts but they became victorious. Esther was an orphan through the death of her parents during the Babylonian captivity. She arose through her cousin, Mordecai, and entered the courts of the king. She found herself in a place where she had favor with the king. Through that favor, she saved an entire nation, her own people. What if she focused on the negativity of her past? What if the abandonment of the past held her in captivity? It would have kept her from being able to step into that place with the king and that resulted in saving the Jews.

Joseph was rejected by all of his brothers and suffered tremendous abuse by their hands. But he did not remain there. He moved on and realized God had a purpose for him though the enemy desired to use that circumstance to defeat him. He became chief advisor to Pharaoh and ended up as a father to Pharaoh. Had his brothers not rejected him and sold him into slavery, the family would not have lived and prospered.

Joseph explained to his brothers: "But now, do not therefore be grieved nor angry with yourselves because you sold me here; for God sent me before you to preserve life. For these two years the famine has been in the land, and there are still five years in which there will be neither plowing nor harvesting. And God sent me before you to preserve a posterity for you in the earth, and to save your lives by a great deliverance. So now it was not you who sent me here, but God; and He has made me a father to Pharaoh, and lord of all his house, and a ruler throughout all the land of Egypt" (Gen. 45:5-8).

When counselors (pastoral or otherwise) are sought out for help we need to engage our faith. We need to simultaneously seek God through His Word and prayer to work through every issue holding us back. The whole purpose of seeking counsel is not only for relief and comfort, but also to be healed so that destiny can be restored and realized.

CHAPTER SEVEN:

THE EFFECTS
OF BREAKING THROUGH
EVERY BARRIER

After my husband's death, my son and daughter-in-law felt I needed company and that I should get a little puppy. A year afterwards I did. My puppy, Missy, taught me about gates and breakthrough. She believed gates were something to be conquered. Although she was a little dog of about ten pounds, she just kept trying to jump the gate between the kitchen and the living room. Finally one day while I was out of town, a friend who was dogsitting came to my home only to find Missy sitting in the living room at the front door waiting for her. Every time after that Missy awaited her at the door. Missy had conquered the gate.

In fact, once she conquered it, the gate was no longer an issue. It did not hold her back. We had to think of a new way to keep her secured in the kitchen. So it is with us. Once we break through a gate, that gate is no longer an issue. A new level of faith is imparted to us and what were once obstacles are now reduced to everyday behavioral expectations. We believe at a new level so we need new challenges. New challenges arise as the old ones have been overcome. But we face these new challenges with a new faith. We go from faith to faith.

The Master of Breakthroughs in the Apostolic Church

The Breaker is upon us. God is more than the Breaker; He is the Master of Breakthroughs (see 2 Samuel 5:20). The apostolic church is breaking through to breaking out. We are on the verge of a joy, boldness, courage, strength, and abandonment falling on the church that no one has experienced in the generations currently on earth. Why? It is because God the Breaker is falling upon His church with a mantle of breakthrough anointing. There are barriers that have been before us all of our lives that suddenly will fall in one day. This is an awesome day to be alive.

Breakthrough Affects the Church in Many Ways

The Breaker brings breakthrough that affects the church in many ways. It is far more than a spiritual experience; it is a physical manifestation of something that has happened in the spiritual dimension. Some people focus on the spiritual happening and others on the physical manifestation. But it is both. In breakthrough, things happen in the natural realm. When we have broken through spiritually, we often read about things happening in the newspapers that we prayed through. Those that focus on the natural often criticize others for being too spiritual while those focusing on spiritual breakthrough often criticize those who seem too practical. But it is both a spiritual and physical event and requires intercession as well as bold action. As we come to new levels of breakthrough, we see that the church is greatly affected in many ways:

We Spread Out

In breakthrough, we begin to spread out. Another word for break out is to spread out. In Micah 2:13, when they broke through the gate, they moved into a larger place and they spread out. The Bible also talks about breaking out of the narrow place. When God comes, we will increase and spread out.

Isaiah 49:19 says, "your waste and your desolate places, and the land of your destruction, shall even now be too narrow by reason of the inhabitants, and they that swallowed you up will be far away." Genesis 28:14 says, "Also your descendants shall be as the dust of the earth; you shall spread abroad to the west and the east, to the north and the south; and in you and in your seed all the families of the earth shall be blessed."

Increase and Blessing

Breaking through and breaking out results in increase as well as blessing. The harvest is released through the Breaker. The church increases numerically, just as in the book of Acts, and begins to spread abroad throughout the earth. This is already happening outside of North America. Churches across Africa, South America, and Asia are being birthed overnight because of the numbers of conversions that are taking place. I have a friend who is an apostle in South Africa and in 3 years his church multiplied to over a thousand and he planted three new churches. To increase in that manner is considered ordinary there.

Increase also directly affects our finances. When the Breaker comes, it releases glory into the church. In Ezekiel, it speaks of the glory being over the threshold. Ezekiel 10:3-4 says, "Now the cherubim were standing on the south side of the temple when the man went in, and the cloud filled the inner court. Then the glory of the Lord went up from the cherub, and paused over the threshold of the temple; and the house was filled with the cloud, and the court was full of the brightness of the Lord's glory."

It is at the threshold that the glory is released. Where the glory is, the presence of the Lord is. Yet it is more than the presence of the Lord that is there. There is an awesome release in the financial realm. Finances are linked with the glory. In Haggai 2:7-9 God said, "I will shake all nations, so that the treasures of all nations shall come in, and I will fill this house with splendor (glory), says the Lord of hosts. The silver is mine, and the gold is mine, says the Lord of hosts. The latter splendor of this house shall be greater than the former, says the Lord of hosts; and in this place I will give prosperity, says the Lord of hosts.'" (RSV)

In the apostolic church in Acts, there was a financial release, as I mentioned earlier in another chapter. When God takes over the church there will not be a financial problem. Generosity marked the breakthrough. When God's church was birthed, finances poured in. Throughout biblical history, prosperity was part of the increase or breakthrough that was upon God's people. In Genesis 30:43, Laban increased exceedingly because the blessing of the Lord was in that house.

Jacob carried the favor and blessing of God. As a result, Laban was blessed and increased.

Revival Breaks Out

Because breakthrough is related to increase, it results in revival. True revival, as outlined by George Otis, Jr. in his book *Informed Intercession*, results in breakthrough. Breakthrough in a city or territory means that whatever was stopping church growth in the heavenlies is broken through and suddenly every church in the territory begins to grow and increase. One church in Cali, Colombia that was around 350 people exploded overnight into 35,000 people when they broke through in 1995.

While in South Africa, a pastor told me this story about the Venda Territory in Northeast South Africa. The territory was ruled by the traditional tribal gods, of which one was the snake god. In the early 1970s an awakening broke out among the young people in the high schools, colleges, and universities. Pastor Khorombi of Venda as well as others were the vanguard of the new movement.[1]

In 1977, Reinhart Bonnke held a crusade in this region. Thousands attended the crusade. It was a turning point in the spiritual landscape of the region. The Breaker came into the crusade. The power of God came in a way that no one had witnessed before in this region. Bonnke waved his hands across the crowd under the anointing of God and multitudes went down under the power of God and had to be carried home. Schools and businesses were shut down for many days because so many people were affected.

The power of darkness that held the region in captivity was broken. A mighty revival broke out and engulfed the entire territory. Nothing has been the same since then. Churches have grown and some are over 1500 in membership. Some of the greatest spiritual leaders in Africa now come from the Venda Territory. The Breaker came into this region and broke through the gate that was holding the people in darkness.

Revelation Explodes

In breakthrough, revelation explodes. We saw in Genesis 28:17 that the church is the gate of heaven. When the gate of heaven is broken through, revelation is part of what is released. Prior to breakthrough, revelation is scarce. First Samuel 3:1 says there was no open vision—no breakthrough vision. Revelation not only releases vision but it releases strategy as to how we are to advance. Revelation will show us the next step to take.

Joy Breaks Out

Breakthrough is marked by joy. The enemy has been overcome at the gates and joy accompanied by singing breaks out. Isaiah 14:7 says, "The whole earth is at rest and quiet; they break forth into singing." Isaiah 44:23 speaks of the eruption that takes place when God breaks out: "Sing, O heavens, for the LORD has done it! Shout, you lower parts of the earth; break forth into singing, you mountains, O forest, and every tree in it! For the Lord has redeemed Jacob, and glorified Himself in Israel."

There is a joy that is being released in this hour that is entirely supernatural. In the last season there were many who ministered the joy of the Lord. People were taught and hands were laid on them at times for the breaking forth of the joy of the Lord. God was restoring joy to His people to renew their strength and restore their souls. It was medicine that flowed from a merry heart, healing them and preparing them for this season.

Something new is happening. There is a breaker anointing that is beginning to be released in joy across the church spontaneously. The purpose of many church services where this is happening may not be to release people into the joy of the Lord. Yet when God comes into a service in this manner, the people will arise and, through their release into joy and shouting, will shut down whatever else is happening. He is delivering His people from captivity, from whatever has held them bound in any manner. An eruption of joy occurs. "When the Lord brought back the captivity of Zion, we were like those who dream. Then our mouth was filled with laughter, and our tongue with singing. Then they said among the nations, 'The Lord has done great things for them.' The Lord has done great things for us, and we are glad" (Ps. 126:1-3).

A supernatural breaking out of joy is beginning to occur. It is the shout of the King in the midst of the people. It is the Breaker breaking in, breaking through, and breaking, and setting us in a new place. Captivity is being turned supernaturally. The Deliverer has come and will continue to come. God is marching into the midst of our church services and when He shows up, He is coming as the triumphant Lion of the Tribe of Judah, the Captain of the Hosts who is leading His people into victory!

New Sound In Worship

With this release, a new sound in worship is leading the way. The breaker anointing is being released over prophetic worship teams across the nation. There are bold new worship leaders who are listening to the sound in heaven (the sound of triumph), and are releasing it on earth. True prophetic worship should lead us into the breaking out on earth of the sound that is in heaven. It is the sound of joy. There is an aspect of apostolic worship that will break out in this season and be multiplied across the nation and throughout the world. It is not the pastoral "Jesus-and-me" kind of worship—it is the sound of triumph. It is our King, our apostolic Leader, leading us in the victory shout.

Part of the breaking through and breaking out will result in the full restoration of the tabernacle of David that includes worship, intercession, and the church itself. There is a remnant church that is about to experience the full restoration of that which God originally intended.

Amos spoke of this in Amos 9:11-12: "'On that day I will raise up the tabernacle of David, which has fallen down, and repair its damages; I will raise up its ruins, and rebuild it as in the days of old; That they may possess the remnant of Edom, and all the Gentiles who are called by My name,' says the Lord who does this thing." Peter repeated it on the Day of Pentecost. I believe that the tabernacle of David is a type of the apostolic church.

The Impenetrable and Immovable Step Aside

Lastly, that which has been impenetrable and immovable is about to be broken through. Psalm 45:2 speaks about breaking in pieces the gates of brass and cutting apart the bars of iron. That which has held back the full manifestation of the presence and power of God is on the way out. There is a church arising on which the Breaker is falling and as a result they are breaking through.

As part of that, the miraculous will break out. Diseases that have not yielded prior to this time are about to bow their knee and break. Terminal and impenetrable diseases are about to flee. I believe we are on the verge of being astounded at

what God can and will do when a people break through and
break out.

Jesus' First Miracle Marked a Breakthrough

Jesus' first miracle at Cana in John 2 represented a breakthrough. Mary, His mother, told the servants to do whatever
Jesus told them to do. Jesus told the servants to fill the pots
with water. He turned that water into wine. Someone had to
take bold action which released faith so the miracle manifested. Jesus broke through again and again in His life. His
resurrection was the ultimate breakthrough in which the
Breaker broke through the gates of death and life broke forth.

Moses and Breakthrough

Furthermore, that which has been unreachable or unattain-
able is about to be ours. Moses and the Israelites are an
example of this. God visited Moses on the backside of the
desert. Moses was banished from the success and prominence
he had in Pharaoh's court as his adopted son. He had lost his
ability to speak and his confidence in his leadership skills.
God met him there in the middle of nowhere and basically
said, "I want you to deliver your people out of Egypt by going
there, confronting Pharaoh and telling him to let My people
go. I will go before you."

Moses raised his human objections to God's challenge.
In the end, Moses listened to God and arose, took Aaron with
him and met with Pharaoh. Transformation had taken place
in Moses' soul and he arose and took his place. Ten times he

and Aaron had to go before Pharaoh to demand that Pharaoh let God's people go. Ten times Pharaoh changed his mind. But Moses would not back down or retreat. He kept going back. He persisted. He would not be denied. This was not his idea; God had spoken to him and he believed God. There was a breakthrough on the way.

As a result, Pharaoh was finally overcome because Moses kept persevering and God kept showing up. The last plague resulted in the death of the firstborn sons of the Egyptians. In that culture, the firstborn son received the double portion. In this last plague is a picture of what God is doing for the church. He is removing the inheritance of the enemy and restoring the firstborn inheritance to the church, the double portion. Israel came out with the spoils or the prosperity of Egypt. This was the portion of Judah also.

In Zechariah 9:11-12 God said through the prophet: "As for you also, because of the blood of your covenant, I will set your prisoners free from the waterless pit. Return to the stronghold, you prisoners of hope. Even today I declare that I will restore double to you."

We Are on the Verge
of Breaking Out

The church in this hour is about to be delivered out of its imprisonment. It will not come out empty-handed but it will come out with the wealth of Egypt and Babylon. God the Breaker, when He breaks open the way, does it with the goods in hand. The church will break through and it will break out. It will not come out empty-handed but it will come out and go forth with a double portion. This is the day of the releasing of all that the double portion represents. It will come out with a double portion in money, businesses, children, anointing, the presence of God, joy, and so on. Abundance is about to break out on the church.

Inheritance Released

Inheritance is another element of the double portion that comes with breakthrough. We have an inheritance in Christ. We are called joint-heirs. This means that when Christ died, an inheritance was released that we are to obtain in this life, not the next. That inheritance that the Apostle Paul spoke about has to do with obtaining the results of who God has called us to be. For instance, part of Paul's inheritance was the Gentiles. When the Gentiles were converted, Paul began to realize his inheritance. Writing the pastoral Epistles was Paul's inheritance. So when those things were accomplished, Paul inherited what was to be his in this life. The manifestation of the gifts of the Spirit are to be part of every believer's inheritance as are the fruit of the Spirit. Prosperity is part of our inheritance. Many have thought that inheritance had to do with when they went to heaven. That is not true. It is for this life, while we are on earth.

God the Breaker loosed the whole nation of Israel out of the control of Egypt through strong and determined apostolic leadership. In these days of the arising of apostolic strength and leadership, whole nations will be freed and loosed to possess their destiny just as Israel was. It will birth nations that have been captive to other powers into freedom, destiny, and increase.

The Breaker is in our midst. It is time to break off lethargy and passivity. Arise and shout and go through the gates, for God the Breaker has already arisen and is going forth before us, breaking open the way! This is the day when all hindrances will shatter into pieces. This is the day when the gates of brass will not resist. I can already hear the gates opening and there is a shout arising and joy breaking forth. This is the breaking forth of the church, the latter day church, with a double portion of the presence and the power of God. This is not a day to weep. This is a day to arise and shout and go forth through the gates. This is the day to possess our inheritance and promise. We will rise up and go through!

Notes
[1] Story verified by Pastor James Ndala of Tzaneen, South Africa.

CHAPTER EIGHT:

THE BIRTH OF
THE APOSTOLIC CHURCH
AT THE GATES

B irthing is a picture of breakthrough. Every birth is a
miracle to the natural eye. Babies form in secret as the
Psalmist said in Psalm 139. We do not know what they will
look like until they arrive. We only know they are coming
and that their coming creates both expectancy as well as great
discomfort for the mother carrying the child. In the ninth
month, the mother becomes desperate. It is as if nothing she
does brings her comfort. The pressure becomes intolerable.
She is restless, uncomfortable, irritable, and without consolation. Only one thing will relieve her—the birthing of the baby.

This child has to go through a very narrow passageway in
order to enter the new place. When God made the human
race, He designed woman so that her body would release a
chemical substance at the time of birth. This substance directly affects the birth canal and causes it to open. That which
has been tightly shut and holds the baby in, at the time of

birth, begins to dilate. There is a season for it to remain shut until the baby is fully formed. But there is a time for the birth canal to open and release that which has been made ready, a beautiful infant child. The birth canal is a gate, a narrow place through which the baby must traverse to find its freedom and full identity and expression. So it is for the church.

Breakthrough of the Church: A Picture of Birthing

God has already created the way for the church to pass through the gates, breaking into the new. He already has "chemicals" ready to release—His power and anointing—which will cause the church to pass through and break out. The gates of hell will not prevail for the end-time apostolic church. We will possess our enemies at the gates. The battle is about to turn at the gates, for there is one who is breaking through, Christ's body on earth. Jesus Christ, the Head, is in heaven. But Jesus Christ, His body, is on earth.

Ephesians 1:18-23 speaks about this. Paul prayed that "the eyes of your understanding being enlightened; that you may know what is the hope of His calling, what are the riches of the glory of His inheritance in the saints, and what is the exceeding greatness of His power toward us who believe, according to the working of His mighty power which He worked in Christ when He raised Him from the dead and seated Him at His right hand in the heavenly places, far above all principality and power and might and dominion, and every name that is named, not only in this age but also in that which is to come. And He put all things under His feet, and *gave Him to be head* over all things *to the church, which is*

His body, the fullness of Him who fills all in all" (emphasis mine).

One Purpose of the Apostolic Church

In Ephesians 3:10-12 Paul set forth one of the purposes of the apostolic church: "that now the manifold wisdom of God might be made known by the church to the principalities and powers in the heavenly places, according to the eternal purpose which He accomplished in Christ Jesus our Lord, in whom we have boldness and access with confidence through faith in Him." This requires a bold, nonreligious, untraditional, free, unencumbered, radical body of people.

The apostolic church has been in the birth canal. This is the day of the restoration of apostolic and prophetic leadership in the church. It is the day of releasing people into an apostolic anointing of bold, overcoming faith and action. For the church to arise out of lethargy, despair, and hopelessness, we need leaders who will arise and lay hold of the prophetic breath and word for the church. Fresh life, energy, excitement, purpose, and vision will permeate the church because prophets are getting and releasing the word of the Lord.

The Place of Decision

We are at a place of decision-making. Bold apostolic and prophetic leaders are arising. People are making daring, faith-filled decisions at the gates. There is a new company arising who understands and sees the battle at the gates. This is a company which, though assailed on every side by discouraging and despairing words and experiences from the past, will arise and press into the Word and prayer. They will do this until the prophetic wind and word of God are released which will overturn death, despair, and hopelessness. That revelatory word from God will propel them forward, causing them to overcome at every narrow place. It will release strategy and direction for the future.

A Nation at the Gates: Baal-Perazim Is About to Break Out

Part of the challenge facing the church today is for leaders to emerge in our cities who will lead the church into bold actions that result in redeeming our cities. We need apostolic leadership and the prophetic wind to blow upon us and begin to birth the word for breakthrough at the gates. Nothing is impossible to God. We are at the gates in North America.

There is a bold leadership arising who will not be afraid to lead. They will arise out of a pastoral mentality to an apostolic mentality that breaks through the gates of unbelief, hopelessness, and despair over our cities and country. We are on the verge of seeing the battle turn at the gates. The church is arising as a battering ram that will burst through every gate. Baal-perazim is about to manifest in the personal lives of people, in our cities and nation.

I understand from some friends who have studied Hebrew that Isaiah 59:29 should read this way: "When the enemy comes in *like a flood, the Spirit of the Lord will lift up a standard against him.*" The NIV says: "From the west, men will fear the name of the LORD, and from the rising of the sun, they will revere his glory. *For he will come like a pent-up flood* that the breath of the LORD drives along" (emphasis mine). Baal-perazim is about to reveal Himself. When He does, the dam will break and the floodwaters of the Lord will carry away every opposing force. God is the Master of the Breakthrough. He is God the Breaker.

The Power of the Prophetic Wind

When the prophetic wind is loosed, faith will arise and God the Breaker will loose everyone and everything stuck at the gates. Arise, O prophetic wind of God! Blow upon your people! Blow through the mouth of the prophets, the authority of the apostles, and begin to blow away the "stuff" which has caused them to get stuck at the gates!

There is a boldness and strength about to come on apostles that will cause them to take their place as bold leaders of churches, cities, and nations leading them into victory. No longer will they be mired in consensus decisions. They will arise because they have heard and they believe.

There is a boldness about to come on the prophets that will astound this nation and turn the heads of top governmental leaders. It will even turn the head of the nation. Prophets who have an Elijah spirit and are unafraid of Jezebel are about to arise and cast her off the walls. No longer will there be an Ahab spirit in the church and nation that is afraid to confront wrong. This nation is on the verge of seeing the apostolic church birthed at the gates. The apostolic church will possess at the gates.

There is a whirlwind of the prophetic that is about to blow that will cause the army to arise out of the place of

death because of lost vision. They will arise and become a
mighty army and no one will be able to stop them.

Davidic Army Arising

As the wind begins to blow, even those who have been cap-
tured at the gates in hopelessness and despair will arise out of
the place of death and push forward with a faith they never
knew possible. This is not a day of defeat. We are on the
verge of the greatest victories we have ever seen. David's
army, the apostolic church, is arising and it is on David's throne
that Jesus sits. So it is the throne of David, the one who overcame the last enemies of God, on which we sit. And David's
throne is forever. We are on the verge of becoming the mighty
army, terrible with banners spoken about in the Song of
Solomon.

This is the day to arise and sing, take down our harps from
the willow tree, and begin to dance and sing the song of victory. It is the time to return to that which God promised us
long ago that has seemed out of reach. It is time to repossess
that which we lost for a season. This is the time for the restoration of the church, of leadership in and for the church, and
of the city in which it resides.

We are at the gates and will break through them! No longer
will we be hindered by adverse circumstances and powers.
Apostles and prophets are arising and together will break
through. Prophets will perceive and boldly declare the word
of the Lord that releases direction and life. Apostles will begin to authoritatively move the church forward through bold
action which releases great power. Both will release awesome angelic intervention through faith-filled declarations.
Together they are about to become the battle-axe that will

break through every barrier. Jeremiah said: "You are My battle-ax and weapons of war: for with you I will break the nation in pieces; with you I will destroy kingdoms" (Jer. 51:20).

"The breaker goes up before them; they break out, pass through the gate, and go out by it. So their king goes on before them, and the LORD at their head" (Micah 2:13, NAS). Boldly arise, O people of God, and break forth into all that God has for us to possess in this hour!

SUBJECT INDEX